WINTER

SEASONS OF THE YEAR

by
Harriet
Brundle

WINDMILL
BOOKS

New York

SEASONS OF THE YEAR

Published in 2018 by **Windmill Books**, an Imprint of Rosen Publishing
29 East 21st Street, New York, NY 10010

Written by: Harriet Brundle
Edited by: Gemma McMullen
Designed by: Ian McMullen

Photo credits: Abbreviations: l-left, r-right, b-bottom, t-top, c-center, m-middle. All images are courtesy of Shutterstock.com. Front Cover – FamVeld. 1, 24 – ISchmidt. 2 - Daniel J. Rao. 3 - Jeka. 4l Konstanttin. 4lc – digis. 4rc – Smileus. 4r – Triff. 5 - Pressmaster. 7 - Halfbottle. 7 - LilKar. 8 - Algefoto. 8inset - Amy Johansson. 9 - Nadezda Cruzova. 9inset - Robsonphoto. 10 - Glenn Young. 10inset - AlinaMD. 11 - fotografos. 12 - rootstock. 13 - Nemeziya. 14 - Air Images. 15 - oliveromg. 16l - chanwangrong. 16c - Christian Delbert. 16r - D7INAMI7S. 17 - Ildi Papp. 17inset - Mindy w.m. Chung. 18 - Alena Ozerova. 19 - ZouZou. 20 - Pressmaster. 21 - Sergey Peterman. 21bl - Wollertz. 21br - SamKent12. 22 - Elovich. 23 - Volodymyr Goinyk.

Cataloging-in-Publication Data
Names: Brundle, Harriet.
Title: Winter / Harriet Brundle.
Description: New York : Windmill Books, 2018. | Series: Seasons of the year | Includes index.
Identifiers: ISBN 9781499484168 (pbk.) | ISBN 9781499484120 (library bound) | ISBN 9781499483963 (6 pack)
Subjects: LCSH: Winter--Juvenile literature. | Seasons--Juvenile literature.
Classification: LCC QB637.8 B78 2017 | DDC 508.2--dc23

Manufactured in the United States of America

CPSIA Compliance Information: Batch #BS17WM: For Further Information contact
Rosen Publishing, New York, New York at 1-800-237-9932

Contents

Words that appear in **bold** can be found in the glossary on page 24.

Seasons of the Year

There are four seasons in a year. The seasons are called spring, summer, fall, and winter.

Each season is different. This book will tell you about winter!

Winter

Winter happens after fall. The winter months are December, January, February, and March.

January

Sun	Mon	Tue	Wed	Thu	Fri	Sat
	2	3	4	5	6	7
9	10	11	12	13	14	
16	17	18	19	20	21	
23	24	25	26	27	28	
30	31					

February

Sun	Mon	Tue	Wed	Thu	Fri	Sat
			1	2	3	4
6	7	8	9	10	11	
13	14	15	16	17	18	
20	21	22	23	24	25	
27	28	29				

March

Sun	Mon	Tue	Wed	Thu	Fri	Sat
			1	2	3	
5	6	7	8	9	10	
12	13	14	15	16	17	
19	20	21	22	23	24	
26	27	28	29	30	31	

April

Sun	Mon	Tue	Wed	Thu	Fri	Sat
1	2	3	4	5	6	7
8	9	10	11	12	13	14
15	16	17	18	19	20	21
22	23	24	25	26	27	28
29	30					

May

Sun	Mon	Tue	Wed	Thu	Fri	Sat
		1	2	3	4	5
6	7	8	9	10	11	12
13	14	15	16	17	18	19
20	21	22	23	24	25	26
27	28	29	30	31		

June

Sun	Mon	Tue	Wed	Thu	Fri	Sat
					1	2
4	5	6	7	8	9	
11	12	13	14	15	16	
18	19	20	21	22	23	
25	26	27	28	29	30	

July

Sun	Mon	Tue	Wed	Thu	Fri	Sat
1	2	3	4	5	6	7
8	9	10	11	12	13	14
15	16	17	18	19	20	21
22	23	24	25	26	27	28
29	30	31				

August

Sun	Mon	Tue	Wed	Thu	Fri	Sat
			1	2	3	4
5	6	7	8	9	10	11
12	13	14	15	16	17	18
19	20	21	22	23	24	25
26	27	28	29	30	31	

September

Sun	Mon	Tue	Wed	Thu	Fri	Sat
						1
2	3	4	5	6	7	8
9	10	11	12	13	14	15
16	17	18	19	20	21	22
23	24	25	26	27	28	29
30						

October

Sun	Mon	Tue	Wed	Thu	Fri	Sat

November

Sun	Mon	Tue	Wed	Thu	Fri	Sat

December

Sun	Mon	Tue	Wed	Thu	Fri	Sat

There are less hours of sunshine in the winter than in any other season. This makes the daytime feel shorter.

The Weather

The weather is very cold in the winter. It is wet and windy.

Frost

Sometimes there is snow in the winter.
It feels very cold to touch.

Be careful
not to slip
on ice!

Plants

Some plants die in the winter. The weather is too cold for them to stay alive.

Branches

Trunk

Most trees lose their leaves.
We can see their trunks and branches.

Animals

Some animals **migrate** in the winter.
Birds fly to places that are warmer.

Other animals **hibernate** in the winter. They find a safe place and sleep through the cold weather.

13

In the Backyard

When there is snow,
we can ride **sleds** outside!

We can make a snowman with our family. It can have a carrot for a nose!

15

Food

Lots of vegetables are ready to be eaten in winter.

Which other vegetables do you like to eat in the winter?

Broccoli

Carrots

Onions

We can use winter vegetables to make meals such as soup and stew.

What Do We Wear in the Winter?

When the weather is cold we need to stay warm. We wear gloves to keep our hands warm.

We also wear a warm coat, a hat, and a scarf.

19

Things to Do in the Winter

In December, many people celebrate Christmas. It is fun to **decorate** a Christmas tree.

We can go to the woods and collect pinecones and chestnuts!

21

Winter Fun

Did you know?

Each snowflake looks different from the next one. Draw yourself playing in the snow!

In some places there is cold weather
all year round! The North Pole and South Pole
are places on Earth where there is always snow.

23

Glossary

Decorate: to add something to an object to make it look better.

Hibernate: to spend the winter sleeping.

Migrate: to move from one place to another.

Sled: an object used to ride over snow.

Index